THE KITCHEN LIBRARY

PUDDINGS & DESSERTS

Carole Handslip

HAMLYN

CONTENTS

This edition published in 1991 by
The Hamlyn Publishing Group Limited,
part of Reed International Books,
Michelin House, 81 Fulham Road,
London SW3 6RB.

© Reed International Books Limited 1980

ISBN 0 600 57215 3

Produced by Mandarin Offset
Printed and bound in Hong Kong

INTRODUCTION

Creating delicious desserts is fun and rewarding. Desserts often bring more compliments than the main course, so the time and effort spent on them is well worthwhile.

Choosing the right dessert to complement the meal is most important. Fresh fruity desserts are the perfect finish to a summer meal. They are usually quick to prepare and cool and refreshing to eat. Light frothy whips and soufflés are ideal to round off a rich meal. Elaborate creamy concoctions taste deliciously decadent after a lighter main course. Pies, puddings and crumbles will satisfy robust appetites, especially in the cold winter months.

Ice cream and frozen desserts are probably the most versatile of all desserts. They can, of course, be prepared well in advance and a stock in the freezer is most useful when unexpected guests arrive. They can be as light and fresh as a fruit sorbet, or as creamy rich as a Bombe au Chocolat and you will find one to suit most menus.

Most desserts can be prepared well in advance and just need a little attention at the last minute – a point well worth remembering whether you are catering for a hungry family or giving a dinner party.

NOTES

Standard spoon measurements are used in all recipes
1 tablespoon = one 15 ml spoon
1 teaspoon = one 5 ml spoon
All spoon measures are level.

Ovens should be preheated to the specified temperature.

For all recipes, quantities are given in both metric and imperial measures. Follow either set but not a mixture of both, because they are not interchangeable.

FRUIT DESSERTS

Tropical Fruit Salad

1 small pineapple
1 x 312 g (11 oz)
  can lychees,
  drained
2 bananas, sliced
1 x 411 g (14½ oz)
  can guavas,
  drained and sliced
2 passion fruit,
  (optional)
250 ml (8 fl oz)
  ginger ale

Cut the pineapple in half lengthways, remove the flesh and cut into pieces, discarding the centre core. Place in a bowl with the lychees, bananas and guavas.

Halve the passion fruit if using, scoop out the flesh and mix with the other fruits. Pour over the ginger ale and chill. Serve with cream if liked.
Serves 8

Caribbean Bananas

4 bananas, halved
   lengthways
75 g (3 oz) soft
   brown sugar
2 tablespoons lemon
   juice
25 g (1 oz) butter
2 tablespoons rum

Place the bananas in an ovenproof dish and sprinkle with the sugar and lemon juice. Dot with the butter and bake in a preheated moderate oven, 180°C (350°F), Gas Mark 4, for 15 minutes.

Arrange the bananas in a warmed serving dish and spoon over the cooking liquor.

Warm the rum in a ladle, ignite and pour over the bananas. Serve flaming, with cream if liked.
Serves 4

Peaches in Blackcurrant Sauce

500 g (1 lb)
  blackcurrants
125 g (4 oz) caster
  sugar
250 ml (8 fl oz)
  water
grated rind and juice
  of 1 orange
6 ripe peaches,
  peeled

Put the blackcurrants, sugar and water in a pan and cook gently, stirring occasionally, until soft. Sieve, pressing as much pulp through as possible. Add the orange rind and juice.

Place the peaches in a serving bowl and pour over the blackcurrant purée. Chill and serve with cream if liked.

Serves 6

Blackcurrant Suedoise

MERINGUE:
2 egg whites
*125 g (4 oz) caster
   sugar*
FRUIT JELLY:
125 g (4 oz) sugar
*150 ml (¼ pint)
   water*
*500 g (1 lb)
   blackcurrants*
*20 g (¾ oz)
   gelatine, soaked in
   4 tablespoons cold
   water*
*150 ml (¼ pint)
   double cream,
   whipped*
*1 teaspoon grated
   chocolate*

Whisk the egg whites until stiff, then whisk in 3 tablespoons of the sugar. Carefully fold in the remaining sugar.

Put the meringue into a piping bag, fitted with a 5 mm (¼ inch) plain nozzle and pipe tiny mounds onto a baking sheet lined with silicone paper. Bake in a preheated cool oven, 150°C (300°F), Gas Mark 2, for 1½ to 2 hours.

Place the sugar and water in a pan. Heat, stirring, until dissolved. Add the blackcurrants and cook gently for 15 minutes. Purée in an electric blender or rub through a sieve.

Place the soaked gelatine in a bowl over a pan of simmering water and stir until dissolved. Add to the purée and leave until beginning to set, stirring occasionally. Pour into a dampened 18 cm (7 inch) soufflé dish and leave in the refrigerator to set.

Turn out onto a plate. Spread the cream over the suedoise and top with meringues. Sprinkle with chocolate.
Serves 6

Summer Pudding

500 g (1 lb) mixed
  redcurrants,
  blackcurrants and
  blackberries
125 g (4 oz) caster
  sugar
250 g (8 oz)
  raspberries
8 slices white bread,
  crusts removed
whipped cream or
  Crémets (see page
  15) to serve

Place the currants and blackberries in a heavy pan with the sugar. Cook gently, stirring occasionally, for 10 to 15 minutes until tender. Add the raspberries and leave to cool. Strain the fruit, reserving the juice.

Cut 3 circles of bread the same diameter as a 900 ml (1½ pint) pudding basin. Shape the remaining bread to fit round the sides of the basin. Soak all the bread in the reserved fruit juice.

Line the bottom of the basin with one of the circles, then arrange the shaped bread around the sides. Pour in half the fruit and place another circle of bread on top. Cover with the remaining fruit, then top with the remaining bread circle.

Cover with a saucer small enough to fit inside the basin and put a 500 g (1 lb) weight on top. Leave in the refrigerator overnight.

Turn onto a serving plate, pour over any remaining fruit juice and serve with whipped cream or crémets.
Serves 8

Apple Snow

500 g (1 lb) cooking
  apples, peeled and
  cored
50 g (2 oz) caster
  sugar
2 tablespoons water
2 egg whites
grated rind and juice
  of ½ lemon
sponge fingers to
  serve

Slice the apples into a pan, sprinkle with the sugar and add the water. Cover and simmer gently for 10 to 15 minutes, then work in an electric blender until smooth or rub through a sieve. Leave to cool.

Whisk the egg whites until stiff and fold into the apple purée with the lemon rind and juice.

Spoon into glasses and serve with sponge fingers.
Serves 4

Apple Mould

175 g (6 oz) sugar
6 tablespoons water
grated rind and juice
 of 1 lemon
1 kg (2 lb) dessert
 apples, peeled and
 cored
50 g (2 oz) glacé
 cherries, chopped
50 g (2 oz)
 preserved ginger,
 chopped
YOGURT SAUCE:
150 ml (¼ pint)
 double cream
150 g (5 oz) natural
 low-fat yogurt
1 tablespoon caster
 sugar

Place the sugar, water, lemon rind and juice in a pan and heat gently, stirring, until dissolved. Bring to the boil and boil for 5 minutes.

Thinly slice the apples into the syrup. Cover and simmer gently for 10 minutes, turning the apples once carefully. Remove the lid and simmer until most of the syrup has evaporated.

Add the cherries and ginger to the pan, cover and leave to cool.

Turn the mixture into a dampened 900 ml (1½ pint) soufflé dish and leave overnight in the refrigerator.

To make the sauce: Whip the cream until it holds its shape then fold in the yogurt and sugar.

Turn the apple mould out onto a plate and serve with the sauce.
Serves 6

Baked Apples with Dates

4 large cooking
  apples
50 g (2 oz) dates,
  stoned and
  chopped
25 g (1 oz) raisins
25 g (1 oz) soft
  brown sugar
½ teaspoon ground
  cinnamon
4 tablespoons cider

Remove the cores from the apples.
Make a shallow cut round the middle
of each one.

Mix together the dates, raisins,
sugar and cinnamon and use to fill
the apple cavities, pressing down
firmly.

Place in an ovenproof dish and add
the cider. Bake in a preheated
moderate oven, 180°C (350°F), Gas
Mark 4, for 50 to 60 minutes, until
soft. Serve hot with cream or
custard.
Serves 4

Apple Amber

500 g (1 lb) cooking
    apples, peeled and
    cored
1 tablespoon water
50 g (2 oz) caster
    sugar
2 egg yolks
grated rind and juice
    of ½ lemon
MERINGUE:
2 egg whites
125 g (4 oz) caster
    sugar

Slice the apples into a pan and add the water and sugar. Cover and cook gently to a pulp, stirring occasionally, then beat until smooth. Beat in the egg yolks, lemon rind and juice and pour into a 600 ml (1 pint) ovenproof dish.

To make the meringue: Whisk the egg whites until stiff. Whisk in 2 tablespoons of the sugar, then fold in the remainder. Pile on top of the apple mixture.

Bake in a preheated moderate oven, 160°C (325°F), Gas Mark 3, for 20 to 30 minutes until golden. Serve hot or cold.
Serves 4

Calvados Apples

125 g (4 oz) sugar
300 ml (½ pint)
  water
6 dessert apples,
  peeled and
  quartered
3 tablespoons
  Calvados or
  brandy
CARAMEL:
75 g (3 oz) sugar
3 tablespoons water
TO SERVE:
brandy snaps

Place the sugar and water in a pan and heat gently, stirring, until dissolved. Bring to the boil, then simmer for 5 minutes. Place the apples in the syrup, cover and simmer gently for 15 to 20 minutes until the apples look clear. Leave to cool in the syrup, then transfer the apples to a glass serving dish.

Boil the syrup rapidly until reduced by about half, then add the Calvados or brandy. Pour over the apples. Leave to cool.

To make the caramel: Place the sugar and water in a pan and heat gently, stirring, until dissolved, then boil rapidly until golden brown. Pour onto an oiled baking sheet and leave to harden. When set, crack into pieces and sprinkle over the apples. Serve with brandy snaps.
Serves 4

Red Fruit Compote

250 g (8 oz) sugar
300 ml (½ pint)
  water
500 g (1 lb)
  blackcurrants
grated rind and juice
  of ½ orange
125 g (4 oz)
  strawberries
125 g (4 oz)
  blackberries
250 g (8 oz)
  raspberries
1 tablespoon
  arrowroot
2 tablespoons port
Crémets (see page
  15) to serve

Place the sugar and water in a pan and heat gently, stirring, until dissolved. Bring to the boil and boil for a few minutes, then add the blackcurrants and orange rind. Simmer gently for 15 minutes until soft.

Strain the fruit, reserving the syrup. Place the blackcurrants in a serving dish and add the remaining fruit.

Return the syrup to the pan and bring to the boil. Mix the arrowroot with the orange juice and stir into the boiling syrup. Cook, stirring, until thickened and clear. Add the port and pour over the fruit. Allow to cool before serving, with crémets.
Serves 8

Crémets

175 g (6 oz) curd
   cheese
1 tablespoon caster
   sugar
170 ml (6 fl oz)
   double cream

Mix the cheese with the sugar, then
gradually beat in the cream. Pile into
a serving dish and chill. Serve with
stewed fruit.
Serves 4 to 6

15

Winter Fruit Salad

*600 ml (1 pint)
   water*
*2 tablespoons clear
   honey*
*2.5 cm (1 inch) piece
   of cinnamon stick*
2 cloves
juice of ½ lemon
*175 g (6 oz) dried
   apricots, soaked
   overnight*
*125 g (4 oz) dried
   prunes, soaked
   overnight*
*125 g (4 oz) dried
   figs, soaked
   overnight*
50 g (2 oz) raisins
*25 g (1 oz) walnut
   halves, coarsely
   chopped*
*25 g (1 oz) flaked
   almonds, toasted*

Place the water, honey, cinnamon and cloves in a pan and bring to the boil. Add the lemon juice. Drain the dried fruits and add to the pan. Cover and simmer gently for 10 minutes.

Add the raisins and simmer for 2 to 3 minutes. Discard the cinnamon and cloves.

Spoon into individual serving dishes and sprinkle with the walnuts and almonds. Serve hot or cold, with cream if liked.

Serves 6

Fruit Chartreuse

900 ml (1½ pints)
  water
200 g (7 oz) sugar
thinly pared rind and
  juice of 3 lemons
2.5 cm (1 inch) piece
  of cinnamon stick
40 g (1½ oz)
  gelatine
4 tablespoons sherry
175 g (6 oz) black
  grapes, seeded
175 g (6 oz) green
  grapes, seeded
150 ml (¼ pint)
  double cream,
  whipped

Put 750 ml (1¼ pints) of the water, the sugar, lemon rind, juice and cinnamon stick in a pan. Heat gently, stirring, until the sugar is dissolved.

Add the gelatine to the remaining water. Leave to soak for 5 minutes, then add to the lemon mixture and heat gently, stirring, until dissolved. Add the sherry and allow to cool slightly. Discard the cinnamon.

Pour a little of the mixture into a 1.2 litre (2 pint) ring mould and chill in the refrigerator until set. Arrange some black grapes on the surface, pour on just enough jelly to cover and leave to set. Add another layer of jelly, leave to set, then arrange green grapes on top. Continue in this way until the mould is full; chill until set.

Turn out onto a serving dish and decorate with piped cream and any remaining grapes.

Serves 6 to 8

Pineapple Romanoff

1 large pineapple
50 g (2 oz) icing
  sugar, sifted
grated rind of
  ½ orange
3 tablespoons
  Curaçao or
  Cointreau
250 g (8 oz)
  strawberries
284 ml (10 fl oz)
  double cream

Cut the pineapple in half lengthways, scoop out the flesh, discarding the central core, and cut into cubes. Reserve the shells. Place the cubes in a bowl with the icing sugar and orange rind. Pour over the Curaçao or Cointreau and leave to soak for 2 hours.

Set aside a few strawberries for decoration; slice the remainder. Whip the cream until it holds its shape, then fold in the sliced strawberries and the pineapple mixture.

Spoon into the pineapple shells, decorate with the reserved strawberries and chill for 30 minutes before serving.

Serves 4 to 6

Pavlova

4 egg whites
250 g (8 oz) caster
    sugar
1 tablespoon
    cornflour
2 teaspoons vinegar
¼ teaspoon vanilla
    essence
FILLING:
284 ml (10 fl oz)
    double cream
2 bananas, sliced
1 small pineapple,
    cut into cubes
2 passion fruit,
    peeled and sliced
2 peaches, peeled and
    sliced

Whisk the egg whites until stiff. Add the sugar, a tablespoon at a time, whisking until the meringue is very stiff. Whisk in the cornflour, vinegar and vanilla.

Pile the meringue onto a baking sheet lined with silicone paper and spread into a 23 cm (9 inch) round. Hollow out the centre slightly and bake in a preheated cool oven, 150°C (300°F), Gas Mark 2, for 1½ hours.

Cool, then remove the paper and place the pavlova on a serving dish. Whip the cream until stiff and fold in some of the fruit. Pile into the pavlova and decorate with the remaining fruit.

Serves 6 to 8

Pears in Red Wine

150 g (5 oz) sugar
150 ml (¼ pint)
  water
150 ml (¼ pint) red
  wine
2.5 cm (1 inch) piece
  of cinnamon stick
6 dessert pears
2 teaspoons
  arrowroot

Place the sugar, water, wine and
cinnamon in a pan. Heat gently until
the sugar is dissolved. Bring to the
boil and boil for 5 minutes.

Peel the pears, leaving on the
stalks, and place in the prepared
syrup. Cover and simmer gently for
20 to 30 minutes until translucent.
Discard the cinnamon stick. Arrange
the pears on a serving dish.

Mix the arrowroot with a little
water, then add to the syrup and
bring to the boil, stirring. Simmer,
stirring, for 1 minute until clear.
Leave to cool. Spoon over the pears
and chill. Serve with whipped cream.
Serves 6

Oranges in Caramel

8 small oranges
250 g (8 oz) sugar
120 ml (4 fl oz) cold
   water
150 ml (¼ pint) hot
   water
brandy snaps to serve

Pare the rind from 1 orange and shred finely. Cook in boiling water for 1 minute, then drain and dry.

Peel the oranges, removing all the pith. Cut into thin slices and hold together with cocktail sticks. Arrange in individual dishes.

Place the sugar and cold water in a pan. Heat gently until dissolved, then boil steadily to a rich brown caramel. Carefully add the hot water and stir until the caramel has melted, heating again if necessary. Leave to cool.

Pour the caramel over the oranges, top with the shredded rind and chill. Serve with brandy snaps.

Serves 4

SOUFFLÉS, MOUSSES & CHARLOTTES

Rich Chocolate Mousse

75 g (3 oz) plain
  chocolate, broken
  into pieces
3 eggs, separated
2 tablespoons sherry
3 tablespoons
  whipped cream
chocolate curls to
  decorate
  (see page 65)

Melt the chocolate in a bowl over a pan of hot water, then add the egg yolks and sherry and mix well.

Whisk the egg whites until fairly stiff then carefully fold into the chocolate mixture. Divide between 4 ramekin dishes and leave in the refrigerator to set.

Pipe a cream rosette on each mousse and top with chocolate curls to serve.

Serves 4

Orange Mousse

4 eggs
2 egg yolks
125 g (4 oz) caster
  sugar
grated rind and juice
  of 1 lemon
15 g (½ oz) gelatine
284 ml (10 fl oz)
  whipping cream,
  whipped
184 g (6½ oz) can
  frozen
  concentrated
  orange juice,
  thawed
finely shredded
  orange rind to
  decorate

Place the eggs, egg yolks, sugar and lemon rind in a bowl and whisk over a pan of hot water until thick and mousse-like. Soak the gelatine in the lemon juice, adding water to make the juice up to 3 tablespoons if necessary.

Place the gelatine and lemon juice in a bowl over a pan of simmering water and stir until dissolved. Fold into the mousse with half the cream and the orange juice.

Stir gently over a bowl of iced water until beginning to set. Pour into a serving bowl and chill until set.

Decorate with piped cream and the orange rind.

Serves 6 to 8

Strawberry Mousse

350 g (12 oz)
   strawberries
2 eggs
1 egg yolk
75 g (3 oz) caster
   sugar
3 tablespoons orange
   juice
15 g (½ oz) gelatine
284 ml (10 fl oz)
   double cream,
   lightly whipped

Set aside a few strawberries for
decoration. Sieve the remainder or
purée in an electric blender, then
sieve to remove pips; there should be
250 ml (8 fl oz) purée.

Place the eggs, egg yolk and sugar
in a bowl and whisk over a pan of
gently simmering water until thick.

Place the orange juice in a small
pan, sprinkle over the gelatine and
leave for 5 minutes. Heat gently to
dissolve the gelatine, then fold into
the egg mousse with the strawberry
purée and half the cream.

Stir over a bowl of iced water until
beginning to set, then turn into a
900 ml (1½ pint) ring mould. Chill
until set.

Turn out onto a serving plate.
Whip the remaining cream until stiff
enough to pipe. Decorate the mousse
with piped cream and the reserved
strawberries.

Serves 8

Chocolate and Orange Mousse

250 g (8 oz) plain
  chocolate, broken
  into pieces
5 tablespoons water
4 eggs
2 egg yolks
75 g (3 oz) caster
  sugar
grated rind and juice
  of 1 orange
15 g (½ oz) gelatine
284 ml (10 fl oz)
  whipping cream,
  whipped
chocolate curls to
  decorate (see
  page 65)

Place the chocolate and water in a small pan and heat gently until melted, then cool.

Whisk the eggs, egg yolks, sugar and orange rind in a bowl over a pan of boiling water, until thick and mousse-like.

Soak the gelatine in the orange juice, adding water to make up to 3 tablespoons if necessary. Place in a bowl over a pan of simmering water and stir until dissolved, then add to the mousse with the chocolate. Stir over a bowl of iced water until thickening, then fold in half the cream and turn into a glass serving bowl.

Decorate with the remaining cream and chocolate curls.

Serves 6 to 8

Mousse Brazilienne

3 eggs
2 egg yolks
75 g (3 oz) caster
  sugar
15 g (½ oz)
  gelatine, soaked in
  3 tablespoons
  strong black coffee
284 ml (10 fl oz)
  whipping cream,
  whipped
125 g (4 oz) praline,
  crushed (see
  page 44)
CARAMEL:
125 g (4 oz) sugar
4 tablespoons water
4 tablespoons hot
  strong black coffee

First make the caramel: Dissolve the sugar in the water over a gentle heat then cook until a rich brown. Carefully add the hot coffee, all at once, stirring until thoroughly blended; reheat to melt the caramel if necessary, then cool.

Place the eggs, egg yolks and sugar in a bowl and whisk over a pan of hot water until thick and mousse-like.

Place the gelatine and coffee mixture in a bowl over a pan of simmering water and stir until dissolved. Fold into the mousse with the whipped cream and the cooled caramel. Stir gently over a bowl of iced water until beginning to set then add the praline.

Pour into a greased 1.75 litre (3 pint) mould and leave to set.

Turn out onto a serving plate and serve with cream if liked.

Serves 8

Chocolate and Chestnut Mould

250 g (8 oz) plain
  chocolate, broken
  into pieces
4 tablespoons water
125 g (4 oz) butter
125 g (4 oz) caster
  sugar
2 x 227 g (8 oz)
  cans unsweetened
  chestnut purée
2 tablespoons brandy
150 ml (¼ pint)
  double cream,
  whipped, to
  decorate

Place the chocolate and water in a small pan and heat gently until melted, then allow to cool.

Cream the butter and sugar together until light and fluffy, then gradually add the chestnut purée, beating well between each addition. Stir in the melted chocolate and brandy. Turn into a greased 900 ml (1½ pint) mould. Leave in the refrigerator overnight.

Turn out onto a serving dish and decorate with piped cream.

Serves 8

Mocha Charlotte

175 g (6 oz) plain
   chocolate, broken
   into pieces
450 ml (³/4 pint)
   strong black coffee
2 eggs, separated
50 g (2 oz) caster
   sugar
15 g (¹/2 oz)
   gelatine, soaked in
   3 tablespoons cold
   water
450 ml (³/4 pint)
   double cream,
   whipped
24 langue de chat
   biscuits
grated chocolate to
   decorate

Place the chocolate in a small pan
with 150 ml (¹/4 pint) of the coffee.
Heat gently until melted, add the
remaining coffee and bring to the
boil, stirring.

Beat the egg yolks and sugar
together until creamy. Stir in the
coffee mixture. Return to the pan
and stir over a gentle heat until the
custard thickens. Add the gelatine and
stir until dissolved. Leave to cool.

Stir over a bowl of iced water until
the mixture starts to thicken, then
fold in two-thirds of the cream.
Whisk the egg whites until stiff and
fold into the mixture. Turn into a
lightly oiled 1.2 litre (2 pint)
Charlotte mould and chill until set.

Turn out onto a plate. Cover the
sides with a thin layer of cream and
press on the biscuits. Top with piped
cream and grated chocolate.
Serves 6 to 8

Charlotte Russe

600 ml (1 pint)
  made lemon jelly,
  cool but liquid
½ glacé cherry
few angelica
  diamonds
16 sponge fingers
CREAM FILLING:
3 egg yolks
25 g (1 oz) caster
  sugar
300 ml (½ pint)
  milk
15 g (½ oz)
  gelatine, soaked in
  3 tablespoons cold
  water
3 drops of vanilla
  essence
250 ml (8 fl oz)
  double cream,
  whipped

Pour a little jelly into a 1.2 litre
(2 pint) Charlotte mould to a depth
of 5 mm (¼ inch) and chill until set.
Arrange the cherry and angelica on
the jelly and set in position with a
little more jelly. Allow the remaining
jelly to set, then chop finely.

Trim one rounded end off the
sponge fingers and arrange to fit
closely around the side of the mould.

To make the filling: Beat the egg
yolks and sugar together until
creamy. Bring the milk to the boil,
then stir into the egg mixture. Stir
over a low heat until thickened.

Strain the custard into a bowl, add
the soaked gelatine and the essence
and stir until dissolved. Cool, then
stir over a bowl of iced water until
the mixture starts to thicken. Fold in
the cream. Pour into the mould,
cover and chill in the refrigerator
overnight.

To serve, invert onto a plate and
arrange the jelly around the base.
Serves 6

Gooseberry Soufflé

500 g (1 lb)
  gooseberries
150 ml (¼ pint)
  water
125 g (4 oz) sugar
2 heads elderflower,
  tied in muslin
  (optional)
4 eggs, separated
75 g (3 oz) caster
  sugar
15 g (½ oz)
  gelatine, soaked in
  3 tablespoons cold
  water
few drops of green
  food colouring
150 ml (¼ pint)
  whipping cream,
  whipped
TO DECORATE:
2 tablespoons
  chopped almonds,
  toasted
4 tablespoons double
  cream, whipped

Tie a band of double greaseproof
paper around a 15 cm (6 inch) soufflé
dish to stand 5 cm (2 inches) above
the rim; oil the inside of the paper.

Place the gooseberries in a pan
with the water, sugar and elderflower,
if using. Cover and simmer gently
for 10 to 15 minutes, until tender.
Remove the elderflower, rub
through a sieve or work in an electric
blender until smooth. Leave to cool.

Place the egg yolks and sugar in a
bowl and whisk over a pan of gently
simmering water until thick.

Place the soaked gelatine in a bowl
over a pan of simmering water and
stir until dissolved. Add to the
gooseberry purée, then carefully fold
into the mousse, with the food
colouring. Fold in the cream.

Whisk the egg whites until stiff;
fold into the mousse when it is
beginning to set. Turn into the
prepared soufflé dish and leave to set
in the refrigerator.

Remove the paper carefully and
press the nuts around the sides.
Decorate with piped cream rosettes.
Serves 6

Lemon Soufflé

3 large eggs,
   separated
175 g (6 oz) caster
   sugar
grated rind and juice
   of 2 lemons
450 ml (¾ pint)
   whipping cream,
   whipped
15 g (½ oz)
   gelatine, soaked in
   3 tablespoons
   water
2 tablespoons
   chopped almonds,
   toasted, to decorate

Tie a band of double greaseproof paper around a 15 cm (6 inch) soufflé dish to stand 5 cm (2 inches) above the rim; oil the inside of the paper.

Place the egg yolks, sugar and lemon rind in a bowl. Heat the lemon juice in a small pan, then pour over the egg mixture. Whisk, using an electric beater, until thick, then fold in two-thirds of the cream.

Stir the soaked gelatine in a bowl over a pan of simmering water until dissolved. Add to the soufflé and stir carefully until beginning to set.

Whisk the egg whites until stiff, then fold into the mixture. Pour into the prepared dish and chill until set.

Remove the paper carefully and press the nuts around the sides. Spread some of the remaining cream over the top and pipe cream around the edge. Chill before serving.
Serves 6 to 8

Soufflé Omelet

4 eggs, separated
2 tablespoons single
  cream
1 tablespoon caster
  sugar
15 g (½ oz) butter
3 tablespoons
  strawberry jam
sifted icing sugar for
  dredging

Place the egg yolks in a bowl with
the cream and sugar and beat well.
Whisk the egg whites until stiff, then
fold into the yolk mixture.

Melt the butter in a 20 cm (8 inch)
omelet pan, then pour in the soufflé
mixture and spread evenly. Cook
over moderate heat for 1 minute
until golden brown underneath.

Put the pan in a preheated
moderately hot oven, 200°C (400°F),
Gas Mark 6, for 3 minutes, or under
a hot grill, until the top is set.

Heat the jam in a small pan. Put
2 skewers in a flame until red hot.

Remove the omelet from the oven
and quickly spread with jam. Fold
over with a palette knife and dredge
thickly with icing sugar. Slide onto a
hot dish and mark a lattice pattern
across the top with the red hot
skewers. Serve immediately.
Serves 2

CREAMS, FOOLS & CUSTARDS

Gooseberry Fool

500 g (1 lb)
 gooseberries
150 g (5 oz) caster
 sugar
2 heads of
 elderflower, tied in
 muslin (optional)
250 ml (8 fl oz)
 whipping cream,
 whipped
few drops of green
 food colouring
langue de chat biscuits
 to serve

Place the gooseberries in a pan with the sugar and the elderflower, if using. Cover and cook for 10 to 15 minutes until tender. Remove the elderflower, and leave to cool. Rub through a sieve or work in an electric blender until smooth.

Fold the cream and colouring into the fruit mixture. Spoon into individual dishes and chill before serving, with langue de chat biscuits.
Serves 6

Banana Whip

4 bananas
1 egg white
25 g (1 oz) caster
 sugar
150 ml (¼ pint)
 double cream,
 whipped
crisp biscuits to serve

Mash the bananas to a smooth purée. Whisk the egg white until stiff, then whisk in the sugar.

Fold the banana purée and meringue into the cream. Spoon into individual dishes and serve immediately, with crisp biscuits.
Serves 4 to 6

Creamed Rice

50 g (2 oz) pudding
  rice
600 ml (1 pint) milk
2 tablespoons caster
  sugar
few drops of vanilla
  essence
150 ml (¼ pint)
  double cream
APRICOT SAUCE:
125 g (4 oz) dried
  apricots, soaked
  overnight in
  450 ml (¾ pint)
  water
75 g (3 oz) caster
  sugar
2 teaspoons lemon
  juice

Place the rice and milk in a pan and bring to the boil, stirring constantly. Simmer gently for 40 minutes or until tender, using a little extra milk if necessary. Add the sugar and vanilla essence and turn into a bowl to cool.

Meanwhile, make the sauce. Simmer the apricots in their soaking water for 15 minutes. Rub through a sieve or work in an electric blender until smooth, then add the sugar and lemon juice.

Lightly whip the cream and fold into the cooled rice. Serve cold with the warm apricot sauce.
Serves 4 to 6

Zabaione

4 egg yolks
75 g (3 oz) caster
  sugar
4 tablespoons
  Marsala
sponge fingers to
  serve

Place the egg yolks in a bowl with the sugar and Marsala. Whisk together over a pan of gently simmering water until thick and mousse-like.

Pour into 4 glasses and serve immediately with sponge fingers.
Serves 4

Prune Whip

250 g (8 oz) prunes,
  stoned
150 g (5 oz) natural
  low-fat yogurt
2 tablespoons clear
  honey
284 ml (10 fl oz)
  double cream,
  whipped
2 tablespoons
  chopped walnuts
  to decorate

Place the prunes in a pan with just enough water to cover and simmer for 15 minutes or until tender. Rub through a sieve or work in an electric blender with 120 ml (4 fl oz) of the cooking water until smooth. Leave to cool.

Fold the prune purée, yogurt and honey into the cream and spoon into individual glass dishes. Decorate with walnuts.
Serves 6 to 8

Honeycomb Mould

2 eggs, separated
50 g (2 oz) caster
    sugar
450 ml (3/4 pint)
    milk
1 teaspoon vanilla
    essence
15 g (1/2 oz)
    gelatine, soaked in
    3 tablespoons cold
    water

Beat the egg yolks and sugar
together until creamy. Bring the
milk to the boil, pour onto the egg
yolk mixture and stir well.

Return to the pan and heat gently,
stirring, until the custard thickens.
Add the essence and soaked gelatine
and stir until dissolved.

Whisk the egg whites until they
form soft peaks. Fold into the
custard. Rinse a 900 ml (1½ pint)
mould with cold water, pour in the
mixture and chill until set.

Turn out onto a plate to serve.
Serves 4

Pêches Brûlée

6 fresh peaches,
    skinned
2 tablespoons
    Cointreau
284 ml (10 fl oz)
    double cream,
    whipped
125 g (4 oz) soft
    brown sugar

Halve the peaches, discard the stones
and place in a shallow ovenproof
dish. Pour over the Cointreau.

Spread the cream over the peaches
to cover them completely and
sprinkle with the sugar. Place under
a preheated hot grill for 3 minutes or
until the sugar has caramelized.

Cool, then chill before serving.
Serves 6

Sherry Trifle

1 packet of trifle
   sponges
3 tablespoons jam
3 egg yolks
2 teaspoons cornflour
25 g (1 oz) caster
   sugar
450 ml (³/4 pint)
   milk
5 tablespoons sherry
2 bananas
150 ml (¹/4 pint)
   double cream,
   whipped
TO DECORATE:
glacé cherries
angelica
blanched almonds,
   toasted

Split the sponge cakes in half, spread
with jam and arrange in a glass
serving bowl.

Beat the egg yolks with the
cornflour and sugar until smooth.
Bring the milk to the boil, pour onto
the egg yolks and stir well.

Return to the pan and heat gently,
stirring constantly, until the mixture
is thick enough to coat the back of a
wooden spoon. Cool slightly.

Sprinkle the sherry over the
sponge cakes and slice the bananas
over the top. Pour over the custard
and leave until set.

Spread a layer of cream over the
top. Decorate with piped cream
rosettes, cherries, angelica and
almonds.

Serves 4

Petits Pots de Chocolat

125 g (4 oz) plain chocolate, broken into pieces
600 ml (1 pint) milk
2 eggs
2 egg yolks
2 tablespoons caster sugar

Place the chocolate in a pan with the milk. Simmer gently for 2 minutes, stirring occasionally. Beat together the eggs, egg yolks and sugar, then pour on the chocolate milk.

Blend well and strain into individual ovenproof china pots or ramekins. Place in a roasting pan, containing 2.5 cm (1 inch) water. Bake in a preheated moderate oven, 180°C (350°F), Gas Mark 4, for 35 to 40 minutes until just set.

Cool and chill before serving.

Serves 4 to 6

Syllabub

grated rind and juice
    of 1 lemon
120 ml (4 fl oz)
    white wine
75 g (3 oz) caster
    sugar
284 ml (10 fl oz)
    double cream
1 egg white
langue de chat
    biscuits to serve

Place the lemon rind and juice in a bowl with the wine and half the sugar. Leave to soak for 1 hour.

Whip the cream until it stands in peaks, then gradually add the wine mixture and continue whipping until it holds its shape.

Whisk the egg white until stiff then whisk in the remaining sugar. Carefully fold into the cream mixture. Spoon into 4 glasses and serve with langue de chat biscuits.
Serves 4

Atholl Brose

40 g (1½ oz)
  almonds, chopped
40 g (1½ oz)
  medium oatmeal
284 ml (10 fl oz)
  double cream
1 tablespoon lemon
  juice
4 tablespoons whisky
3 tablespoons honey
lemon twists to
  decorate

Place the almonds and oatmeal under a preheated medium grill until brown, turning frequently. Leave to cool.

Whip the cream until it stands in soft peaks, then whisk in the lemon juice, whisky and honey.

Fold in the almonds and oatmeal. Spoon into 6 glasses and chill. Decorate with lemon twists before serving.
Serves 6

Apricot Ambrosia

1 x 411 g (14½ oz)
  can apricot halves,
  drained
1 tablespoon honey
50 g (2 oz) ratafias
150 ml (¼ pint)
  double cream,
  whipped
1 tablespoon flaked
  almonds, toasted

Place the apricots and honey in an electric blender and work until smooth.

Break the ratafias into bite-sized pieces. Fold into the whipped cream, together with the apricot purée.

Spoon into 4 glass dishes and chill. Sprinkle with almonds to serve.
Serves 4

Crème Caramel

75 g (3 oz)
  granulated sugar
3 tablespoons water
3 eggs
25 g (1 oz) caster
  sugar
450 ml (¾ pint)
  milk
½ teaspoon vanilla
  essence

Put the granulated sugar and water in a pan. Heat gently, stirring, until dissolved, then cook to a rich caramel without stirring. Carefully add 1 teaspoon of boiling water and pour into a 900 ml (1½ pint) soufflé dish or mould. Leave to set.

Beat the eggs and caster sugar together. Heat the milk almost to boiling point and add to the eggs with the vanilla essence. Mix well. Strain into the soufflé dish and place in a roasting pan containing 2.5 cm (1 inch) water. Bake in a preheated cool oven, 140°C (275°F), Gas Mark 1, for 1½ hours until set. Cool, then turn out onto a serving dish.
Serves 4

ICES & FROZEN DESSERTS

St. Clement's Ice Cream

3 eggs, separated
175 g (6 oz) caster
  sugar
grated rind and juice
  of 1 lemon
grated rind and juice
  of 1 orange
284 ml (10 fl oz)
  double cream,
  whipped

Whisk the egg yolks, half the sugar and the lemon and orange rinds together until thick and creamy. Strain the fruit juices into a pan and heat gently, then pour onto the egg mixture and continue whisking until thick.

Whisk the egg whites until stiff, then whisk in the remaining sugar. Fold into the egg mixture, with the cream.

Turn into a rigid freezerproof container. Cover, seal and freeze until firm.

Scoop into chilled glasses and serve with wafer biscuits if liked.
Serves 6 to 8

Iced Mocha Mousses

3 eggs, separated
75 g (3 oz) caster
    sugar
50 g (2 oz) plain
    chocolate, chopped
1 tablespoon instant
    coffee powder
2 tablespoons water
150 ml (¼ pint)
    double cream,
    whipped
grated chocolate to
    decorate

Whisk the egg yolks with the sugar until thick and creamy.

Place the chocolate, coffee and water in a bowl over a pan of hot water and heat gently until melted, then whisk into the egg mixture. Fold in the cream.

Whisk the egg whites until stiff and carefully fold into the mousse. Pour into individual freezerproof ramekin dishes. Cover, seal and freeze for 3 to 4 hours.

Transfer to the refrigerator 10 minutes before serving to soften. Decorate with grated chocolate.

Serves 4 to 6

Vanilla Ice Cream

2 eggs
2 egg yolks
75 g (3 oz) caster
    sugar
450 ml (¾ pint)
    single cream
2-3 drops of vanilla
    essence
284 ml (10 fl oz)
    double cream,
    whipped
langue de chat or wafer
    biscuits to serve

Mix the eggs, egg yolks and sugar together. Bring the single cream gently to the boil and pour onto the egg mixture, stirring vigorously. Strain, then stir in the vanilla essence. Leave to cool, then fold in the whipped cream.

Pour into a rigid freezerproof container. Cover, seal and freeze for 1 hour. Remove and stir well, then re-freeze until firm.

Transfer to the refrigerator 20 minutes before serving to soften. Scoop into chilled glasses and serve with langue de chat or wafer biscuits.

Serves 8

VARIATIONS:

Chocolate: Break 250 g (8 oz) plain chocolate into pieces and melt with the single cream.

Praline: Place 50 g (2 oz) blanched almonds and 50 g (2 oz) caster sugar in a pan and heat gently until the sugar melts. Cook, stirring, until nut brown. Turn onto an oiled baking sheet and leave until hard. Crush with a rolling pin and add to the custard with the double cream.

Coffee: Dissolve 3 tablespoons instant coffee powder in 2 tablespoons boiling water, cool and add to the custard with the double cream.

Ginger: Finely chop 125 g (4 oz) preserved stem ginger. Add to the eggs and sugar. Add 2 tablespoons of the ginger syrup to the custard with the double cream.

Banana Ice

1 x 426 ml (³/4 pint)
  can evaporated
  milk, chilled
125 g (4 oz) soft
  brown sugar
3 ripe bananas
1 tablespoon lemon
  juice
wafer biscuits to serve

Whisk the evaporated milk until
thick and mousse-like, using an
electric beater if possible, then whisk
in the sugar. Mash the bananas to a
pulp with the lemon juice, then
whisk into the evaporated milk.

Turn into a rigid freezerproof
container. Cover and freeze for 1 hour.
Stir well, then re-freeze until firm.

Transfer to the refrigerator 30
minutes before serving to soften.
Scoop into chilled glasses and serve
with wafer biscuits.
Serves 8

Strawberry Ice Cream

350 g (12 oz)
   strawberries
15 g (½ oz)
   gelatine, soaked in
   3 tablespoons cold
   water
1 x 426 ml (¾ pint)
   can evaporated
   milk, chilled
175 g (6 oz) caster
   sugar
few drops of red food
   colouring
juice of ½ lemon
8 strawberries to
   decorate

Rub the strawberries through a sieve or purée in an electric blender and sieve to remove pips; there should be 300 ml (½ pint) purée.

Place the soaked gelatine in a bowl over a pan of simmering water and stir until dissolved. Add to the strawberry purée.

Whisk the evaporated milk until thick then add the sugar, strawberry purée, colouring and lemon juice. Turn into a rigid freezerproof container. Cover, seal and freeze for 1 hour.

Remove from the freezer and stir well, then re-freeze until solid. Transfer to the refrigerator 1 hour before serving to soften. Scoop into chilled glasses and decorate each with a strawberry.
Serves 8

Pineapple Ice Cream

1 large pineapple
3 egg whites
175 g (6 oz) caster
   sugar
300 ml (½ pint)
   double cream,
   whipped

Cut the pineapple in half lengthwise. Scrape out the flesh and juice into a bowl, discarding the hard core. Chill the shells in the refrigerator; chop the flesh finely or purée in an electric blender.

Whisk the egg whites until stiff then gradually add the sugar, whisking continuously. Fold in the cream and chopped pineapple.

Place in a rigid freezerproof container. Cover, seal and freeze for 1 hour. Remove from the freezer, stir well then re-freeze until solid.

Transfer to the refrigerator 30 minutes before serving to soften. Scoop into the chilled pineapple shells and arrange on a serving dish. Scoop into chilled glass dishes to serve.
Serves 6 to 8

Bombe Noël

50 g (2 oz) glacé
    cherries
50 g (2 oz) angelica
50 g (2 oz)
    crystallized
    pineapple
50 g (2 oz)
    crystallized ginger
50 g (2 oz) raisins
2 tablespoons brandy
2 tablespoons
    Cointreau
3 egg yolks
75 g (3 oz) caster
    sugar
284 ml (10 fl oz)
    single cream
few drops of vanilla
    essence
284 ml (10 fl oz)
    double cream,
    whipped
TO DECORATE:
angelica and
    crystallized
    pineapple

Chop the cherries, angelica,
pineapple and ginger and place in a
bowl. Add the raisins. Pour on the
brandy and Cointreau. Leave to soak
for 1 hour.

Beat the egg yolks and sugar
together until creamy. Bring the
single cream slowly to the boil, then
pour onto the egg mixture, stirring
vigorously. Strain, add the vanilla
and leave to cool.

Fold half the cream and the fruit
into the custard. Place in a rigid
freezerproof container. Cover and
freeze for 1 hour. Remove from the
freezer and stir well. Turn into a 1.5
litre (2½ pint) freezerproof pudding
basin, cover with foil and freeze until
firm.

Dip the basin into cold water and
turn the bombe out onto a chilled
serving plate. Pipe the remaining
cream in rosettes around the bombe
and decorate with diamonds of
angelica and pieces of pineapple.
Serves 6 to 8

Brown Bread Ice Cream

75 g (3 oz)
  wholemeal
  breadcrumbs
50 g (2 oz) demerara
  sugar
50 g (2 oz)
  hazelnuts, skinned
  and ground
3 egg whites
125 g (4 oz) caster
  sugar
450 ml (¾ pint)
  double cream,
  lightly whipped
18 hazelnuts, to
  decorate

Combine the breadcrumbs, demerara sugar and hazelnuts on a heatproof plate. Place under a preheated hot grill until golden brown, stirring occasionally. Leave to cool.

Whisk the egg whites until stiff, then gradually whisk in the caster sugar. Fold two-thirds of the cream into the meringue with the breadcrumb mixture.

Turn into a 1.2 litre (2 pint) freezerproof mould. Cover, seal and freeze until solid.

Turn out onto a plate 30 minutes before serving. Decorate with the remaining cream and the hazelnuts. Leave in the refrigerator to soften until required.
Serves 6 to 8

Blackberry Ice Cream

500 g (1 lb)
    blackberries
2 tablespoons caster
    sugar
120 ml (4 fl oz)
    water
50 g (2 oz)
    granulated sugar
3 egg yolks
450 ml (¾ pint)
    single cream
2 tablespoons icing
    sugar, sifted
2 tablespoons rose
    water
wafer biscuits to
    serve

Put the blackberries in a pan with the caster sugar and simmer gently for 10 minutes or until tender. Rub through a sieve and leave to cool.

Put the water and granulated sugar in a pan and heat gently, stirring, until dissolved. Increase the heat and boil steadily until the syrup reaches a temperature of 110°C (230°F). At this stage a little of the cooled syrup will form a thread when drawn between the thumb and forefinger.

Cool slightly then pour onto the egg yolks, whisking until the mixture is thick and mousse-like. Mix the cream with the fruit purée, icing sugar and rose water and fold into the mousse.

Turn into a rigid freezerproof container. Cover, seal and freeze.

Transfer to the refrigerator 1 hour before serving to soften. Scoop into chilled glasses and serve with wafer biscuits.

Serves 8

Meringue Glacé aux Ananas

MERINGUE:
4 egg whites
*250 g (8 oz) caster
sugar*
FILLING:
*½ quantity Pine-
apple Ice Cream
(see page 46)*
*284 ml (10 fl oz)
double cream*
*50 g (2 oz)
preserved ginger,
thinly sliced*
*2 tablespoons ginger
syrup*
TO DECORATE:
*3 tablespoons double
cream, whipped*
*15 g (½ oz)
preserved ginger,
sliced*

Make the meringue, pipe and cook
three 15 cm (6 inch) rounds as for
Vacherin au Marrons (see page 84).

Remove the pineapple ice cream
from the freezer and allow to thaw
for 10 minutes at room temperature.

Whip the cream until it forms soft
peaks. Fold in the ginger and syrup.

Line a 20 cm (8 inch) cake tin with
a layer of pineapple ice. Place a
meringue round on top and cover
with half the ginger cream. Repeat
these layers and top with the third
meringue round, filling the space at
the sides with pineapple ice cream.
Cover with foil and freeze for 3 to 4
hours.

Transfer to the refrigerator 1 hour
before serving to soften. Turn out
onto a serving dish and decorate
with piped cream and ginger.
Serves 8

Bombe au Chocolat

CHOCOLATE ICE
CREAM:
2 eggs
2 egg yolks
*75 g (3 oz) caster
sugar*
*450 ml (³/4 pint)
single cream*
*250 g (8 oz) plain
chocolate, chopped*
*284 ml (10 fl oz)
double cream*

FILLING:
1 tablespoon rum
*1 tablespoon icing
sugar*
*150 ml (¹/4 pint)
double cream,
whipped*
3 bananas, sliced

Make the chocolate ice cream (see page 44) and freeze until firm.

Add the rum and icing sugar to the cream and fold in the bananas.

Line the sides of a chilled 1.5 litre (2½ pint) bombe mould or freezerproof basin thickly with the chocolate ice cream. Fill the centre with the banana filling and cover with any remaining ice cream. Put on the lid of the bombe mould or cover the basin with foil and freeze for 4 hours.

Dip the mould or basin into cold water and turn the bombe out onto a chilled serving dish.
Serves 6 to 8

Mint Water Ice

450 ml (¾ pint)
  water
125 g (4 oz) sugar
thinly pared rind and
  juice of 2 lemons
25 g (1 oz) mint
  leaves
few drops of green
  food colouring
1 egg white
TO DECORATE:
small mint leaves
caster sugar for
  sprinkling

Put the water, sugar, lemon rind and juice in a pan and heat gently, stirring, until the sugar is dissolved. Bring to the boil and simmer for 5 minutes, then add the mint leaves, cover and leave to cool. Strain and add the colouring. Turn into a rigid freezerproof container. Cover, seal and freeze.

When half-frozen, whisk most of the egg white until stiff and fold into the water ice. Cover, seal and freeze until firm.

Brush the small mint leaves with the reserved egg white. Sprinkle with sugar and leave to dry for about 1 hour.

Transfer the ice to the refrigerator 10 minutes before serving to soften. Scoop into chilled glasses and decorate with sugared mint leaves.
Serves 6

Blackcurrant Water Ice

500 g (1 lb)
  blackcurrants
150 ml (¼ pint) +
  2 tablespoons
  water
125 g (4 oz) caster
  sugar
juice of ½ lemon
1 egg white, lightly
  whisked

Place the blackcurrants in a pan with 2 tablespoons of the water and simmer until tender. Rub through a sieve or purée in an electric blender; there should be 300 ml (½ pint) purée.

Place the sugar and remaining water in a pan and heat gently, stirring until dissolved. Bring to the boil and simmer for 5 minutes; allow to cool. Add to the blackcurrant purée with the lemon juice. Turn into a rigid freezerproof container. Cover, seal and freeze.

When half-frozen, fold in the egg white. Freeze until firm. Transfer to the refrigerator 10 minutes before serving to soften. Scoop into chilled glasses.
Serves 4

Orange Sorbet

450 ml (³/4 pint)
   water
75 g (3 oz) sugar
thinly pared rind and
   juice of 1 lemon
184 g (6¹/2 oz) can
   frozen
   concentrated
   orange juice,
   thawed
1 egg white

Place the water, sugar, lemon rind
and juice in a pan and heat gently,
stirring until dissolved. Bring to the
boil, simmer for 5 minutes, then
allow to cool.

Remove the lemon rind and add
the orange juice. Turn into a rigid
freezerproof container. Cover, seal
and freeze.

When half-frozen, whisk the egg
white and fold into the sorbet.
Return to the freezer; stir once or
twice during freezing.

Transfer to the refrigerator 10
minutes before serving to soften.
Scoop into chilled glasses.
Serves 6

Raspberry Parfait

500 g (1 lb)
  raspberries
2 egg whites
125 g (4 oz) caster
  sugar
284 ml (10 fl oz)
  double cream,
  lightly whipped
1 tablespoon
  Cointreau
crisp biscuits to serve

Rub the raspberries through a sieve or work in an electric blender until smooth and sieve to remove pips. Place in a rigid freezerproof container. Cover, seal and freeze for 1 to 2 hours, until half-frozen.

Whisk the egg whites until stiff. Whisk in the sugar, a tablespoon at a time; the mixture should be very stiff.

Beat the half-frozen purée with a fork. Fold the cream into the egg white mixture, then carefully fold in the half-frozen purée and the Cointreau.

Spoon into chilled glasses and serve immediately with crisp biscuits.

Serves 4 to 6

Bombe Grand Marnier

450 ml (³/4 pint)
  double cream
150 ml (¹/4 pint)
  single cream
100 g (4 oz)
  meringues
2 tablespoons Grand
  Marnier
1 tablespoon icing
  sugar, sifted
TO DECORATE:
150 ml (¹/4 pint)
  double cream
finely shredded
  orange rind,
  blanched and dried

Whip the double and single creams together until the mixture forms soft peaks. Break the meringues into pieces and fold into the cream, together with the Grand Marnier and icing sugar. Turn into a 1.2 litre (2 pint) freezerproof pudding basin, cover with foil and freeze until firm.

Turn out onto a serving dish 45 minutes before serving. Decorate with piped cream rosettes and orange rind shreds. Leave in the refrigerator until required.

Serves 8

Avocado Ice Cream

2 ripe avocados,
    peeled and stoned
150 ml (¼ pint)
    single cream
284 ml (10 fl oz)
    double cream
75 g (3 oz) caster
    sugar
juice of ½ lemon
50 g (2 oz) split
    almonds, finely
    chopped and
    toasted

Place the avocados and single cream in an electric blender and work until smooth.

Whip the double cream until it forms soft peaks. Fold in the sugar, avocado mixture, lemon juice and almonds. Place in a rigid freezerproof container. Cover, seal and freeze.

Transfer to the refrigerator 30 minutes before serving to soften. Scoop into 4 chilled glasses.
Serves 4

Treacle Tart

SHORTCRUST PASTRY:
175 g (6 oz) plain flour
75 g (3 oz) butter or margarine
1-2 tablespoons iced water

FILLING:
250 g (8 oz) golden syrup
75 g (3 oz) fresh white breadcrumbs
grated rind of ½ lemon

Sift the flour into a bowl. Rub in the butter or margarine until the mixture resembles fine breadcrumbs. Add the water gradually and mix to a firm dough.

Turn out onto a floured surface and knead lightly. Roll out thinly to a 23 cm (9 inch) circle. Use to line an 18 cm (7 inch) flan ring placed on a baking sheet. Chill the flan and pastry trimmings for 15 minutes.

Mix the syrup, breadcrumbs and lemon rind together and spread over the pastry. Roll out the trimmings, cut into long narrow strips and make a lattice pattern over the filling.

Bake in a preheated moderately hot oven, 200°C (400°F), Gas Mark 6, for 30 to 35 minutes. Serve warm with cream.
Serves 4 to 6

Lemon Meringue Pie

175 g (6 oz)
  shortcrust pastry
  (see opposite)
4 tablespoons
  cornflour
300 ml (½ pint)
  water
25 g (1 oz) butter
grated rind and juice
  of 2 small lemons
2 eggs, separated
175 g (6 oz) caster
  sugar

Roll out the pastry and use to line a 20 cm (8 inch) fluted flan ring. Line with greaseproof paper and dried beans and bake in a preheated moderately hot oven, 200°C (400°F), Gas Mark 6, for 15 to 20 minutes. Remove paper and beans and return to the oven for 5 minutes. Remove the flan ring and cool on a wire rack.

Blend the cornflour with a little of the water in a small pan. Add the remaining water and the butter. Bring to the boil slowly, stirring constantly. Cook, stirring, for 3 minutes. Remove from the heat and add the lemon rind and juice, egg yolks and 50 g (2 oz) of the sugar. Pour into the flan case.

Whisk the egg whites until very stiff, then whisk in 50 g (2 oz) of the sugar. Fold in the remaining sugar and spread over the filling.

Bake in a preheated moderate oven, 160°C (325°F), Gas Mark 3, for 20 to 25 minutes. Serve hot or cold.
Serves 4 to 6

Spiced Apple Pie

750 g (1½ lb)
  cooking apples,
  peeled, cored and
  thinly sliced
75 g (3 oz) soft
  brown sugar
½ teaspoon ground
  cinnamon
½ teaspoon grated
  nutmeg
4 cloves
175 g (6 oz)
  shortcrust pastry
  (see page 56)
water and caster
  sugar to glaze
CRÈME À LA
  VANILLE:
2 egg yolks
1 teaspoon cornflour
25 g (1 oz) caster
  sugar
300 ml (½ pint)
  milk
½ teaspoon vanilla
  essence

Layer the apples with the sugar and spices in a 900 ml (1½ pint) pie dish, finishing with a layer of apples.

Roll out the pastry thinly to a circle about 5 cm (2 inches) larger than the pie dish. Cut off a narrow strip all round and use to cover the dampened rim of the pie dish; brush with water.

Lift the pastry onto the rolling pin and place over the apples, sealing the edges well. Trim and flute the edges; make a hole in the centre.

Brush with water, sprinkle with sugar and bake in a preheated hot oven, 200°C (400°F), Gas Mark 6, for 30 to 40 minutes.

To make crème à la vanille: Cream the egg yolks with the cornflour and sugar. Bring the milk to the boil, pour onto the egg yolk mixture and stir well.

Return to the pan and heat gently, stirring constantly, until the mixture is thick enough to coat the back of a spoon. Add the essence then strain.

Serve the pie hot or cold with the crème à la vanille handed separately.
Serves 4 to 6

French Apple Flan

PÂTE SUCRÉE:
*175 g (6 oz) plain
  flour*
75 g (3 oz) butter
*75 g (3 oz) caster
  sugar*
3 egg yolks
*few drops of vanilla
  essence*
FILLING:
*1.5 kg (3 lb) cooking
  apples, peeled and
  thinly sliced*
*50 g (2 oz) caster
  sugar*
GLAZE:
*4 tablespoons apricot
  jam*
juice of ½ lemon

Sift the flour onto a marble slab or
cool work surface. Make a well in
the centre and in it place the butter,
sugar, egg yolks and essence. Using
the fingertips of one hand, work
these ingredients together, then draw
in the flour. Knead lightly until
smooth and chill for 1 hour.

Roll out the pastry very thinly and
use to line a 25 cm (10 inch) fluted
flan ring. Fill the case generously
with apples, then arrange an
overlapping layer of apples on top.
Sprinkle with the sugar. Bake in a
preheated moderately hot oven,
190°C (375°F), Gas Mark 5, for 35 to
40 minutes.

Meanwhile, heat the jam with the
lemon juice, then strain and brush
over the apples. Serve hot or cold,
with cream.
Serves 8

Mince Pies

RICH SHORTCRUST PASTRY:
250 g (8 oz) plain flour
150 g (5 oz) butter
1 tablespoon caster sugar
1 egg yolk
1-2 tablespoons cold water
milk to glaze
FILLING:
4-5 tablespoons mincemeat
1 tablespoon brandy
TO SERVE:
sifted icing sugar

Sift the flour into a bowl and rub in the butter until the mixture resembles breadcrumbs. Stir in the sugar. Add the egg yolk and enough water to mix to a firm dough. Knead lightly and chill for 15 minutes.

Roll out half the pastry fairly thinly on a floured surface and cut out 10 to 12 rounds, using a 6 cm (2½ inch) fluted cutter. Roll out the other half of the pastry a little thinner than the first, cut out 7.5 cm (3 inch) rounds and use to line 10 to 12 patty tins.

Mix the mincemeat with the brandy and divide between the patty tins. Dampen the edges of the pastry, place the smaller rounds on top and press the edges together. Make a hole in the centre of each and brush with milk.

Bake in a preheated moderately hot oven, 200°C (400°F), Gas Mark 6, for 15 to 20 minutes until golden. Sprinkle with icing sugar and serve warm.
Makes 10 to 12

Mincemeat Flan

250 g (8 oz) rich
    shortcrust pastry
    (see opposite)
water and caster
    sugar to glaze
FILLING:
500 g (1 lb)
    mincemeat
2 dessert apples,
    peeled, cored and
    chopped
125 g (4 oz) grapes,
    halved and seeded
grated rind of 1 orange
2 tablespoons brandy
TO SERVE:
1 tablespoon brandy
150 ml (¼ pint)
    double cream,
    whipped

Roll out two-thirds of the pastry
thinly on a floured surface and use to
line a 23 cm (9 inch) fluted flan ring.
Chill the flan and remaining pastry
for 15 minutes.

Mix the filling ingredients
together and use to fill the flan case.

Roll out the remaining pastry
thinly and cut out about twelve
7.5 cm (3 inch) rounds, with a fluted
cutter. Dampen the edges of the
pastry in the flan ring and arrange
the rounds overlapping around the
edge.

Brush with water, sprinkle with
caster sugar and bake in a preheated
moderately hot oven, 200°C (400°F),
Gas Mark 6, for 35 to 40 minutes
until golden.

Fold the brandy into the cream.
Serve the flan hot or cold, topped
with the brandy cream.
Serves 6 to 8

Blackcurrant Flan

PASTRY:
175 g (6 oz) plain flour
2 teaspoons ground cinnamon
125 g (4 oz) butter
25 g (1 oz) caster sugar
1 egg yolk
2 teaspoons water
water and caster sugar to glaze
FILLING:
500 g (1 lb) blackcurrants
125 g (4 oz) demerara sugar

Sift the flour and cinnamon together into a bowl. Rub in the butter until the mixture resembles breadcrumbs. Stir in the caster sugar. Add the egg yolk and water and mix to a firm dough.

Knead lightly, then roll out thinly on a floured surface and use to line an 18 cm (7 inch) flan ring. Chill the flan and pastry trimmings for 15 minutes.

Put the blackcurrants and demerara sugar in a pan. Cover and cook gently for 10 minutes, then uncover, increase the heat and cook until thick and syrupy. Turn onto a plate to cool.

Place the fruit in the flan case. Roll out the pastry trimmings, cut into strips and make a lattice pattern over the fruit. Brush with water and sprinkle with caster sugar.

Bake in a preheated moderately hot oven, 200°C (400°F), Gas Mark 6, for 25 to 30 minutes, until golden.

Serve warm or cold, with whipped cream.
Serves 4 to 6

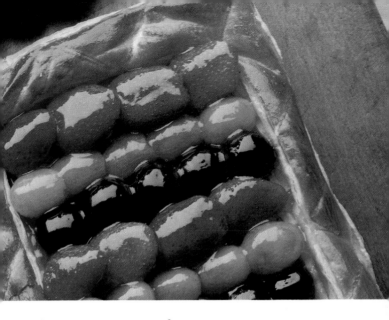

Tarte Française

*1 x 368 g (13 oz)
  packet frozen puff
  pastry, thawed*
*1 egg yolk, mixed
  with 1 teaspoon
  water*
GLAZE:
*4 tablespoons apricot
  jam*
2 tablespoons water
*1 teaspoon lemon
  juice*
FILLING:
*125 g (4 oz) black
  grapes, seeded*
*125 g (4 oz) green
  grapes, seeded*
*125 g (4 oz)
  strawberries*

Roll out the pastry to a rectangle,
about 30 x 20 cm (12 x 8 inches).
Sprinkle the pastry lightly with flour
and fold in half lengthways.

Cut out a rectangle from the
folded edge, leaving a 3.5 cm
(1½ inch) wide band on the
remaining 3 sides.

Open out the rectangle and roll
out until 30 x 20 cm (12 x 8 inches).
Place on a dampened baking sheet,
prick all over and dampen the edges.

Open out the band of pastry and
place on the rectangle to make a
border. Knock up the edges and
mark a pattern on the border with a
knife. Brush the border with the egg
yolk and water and bake in a
preheated hot oven, 220°C (425°F),
Gas Mark 7, for 20 to 25 minutes
until golden brown.

Heat the jam with the water and
lemon juice then sieve and reheat.
Use to brush the base of the pastry
case, then arrange the fruit in rows
down the tart. Brush generously
with the glaze. Serve cold.
Serves 6

Baked Cheesecake

75 g (3 oz) butter
125 g (4 oz) caster
  sugar
grated rind and juice
  of 1 lemon
300 g (10 oz) curd
  cheese
2 eggs, separated
50 g (2 oz) ground
  almonds
25 g (1 oz) semolina
50 g (2 oz) sultanas
sifted icing sugar for
  dredging

Cream the butter, sugar and lemon rind together until light and fluffy. Beat in the cheese gradually, then mix in the egg yolks and beat thoroughly. Add the almonds, semolina, sultanas and lemon juice and mix well. Whisk the egg whites until stiff and carefully fold into the cheese mixture.

Spoon into a lined and greased 20 cm (8 inch) loose-bottomed cake tin and bake in a preheated moderate oven, 180°C (350°F), Gas Mark 4 for 50 to 60 minutes. Turn off the heat and leave the cheesecake in the oven until cold.

Turn out and sprinkle with icing sugar.
Serves 6 to 8

Chocolate Cheesecake

50 g (2 oz) butter, melted
150 g (5 oz) digestive biscuits, finely crushed
50 g (2 oz) demerara sugar
175 g (6 oz) plain chocolate
1 x 227 g (8 oz) carton cream cheese
75 g (3 oz) caster sugar
2 eggs, separated
284 ml (10 fl oz) double cream, lightly whipped
chocolate curls to decorate (see note)

Combine the butter, biscuit crumbs and demerara sugar. Press the mixture over the base and sides of a 23 cm (9 inch) loose-bottomed flan tin and place in the refrigerator to harden.

Melt the chocolate in a bowl over a pan of hot water. Blend the cheese, caster sugar and egg yolks together, then mix in the chocolate. Fold in half the cream.

Whisk the egg whites until stiff and fold into the mixture. Turn into the crumb case and leave in the refrigerator to set.

Whip the cream until stiff enough to pipe. Decorate the cheesecake with piped cream and chocolate curls.

Serves 6

NOTE: To make chocolate curls, shave thin layers from a block of chocolate, using a potato peeler.

PUDDINGS

Treacle Pudding

125 g (4 oz) butter
  or margarine
125 g (4 oz) caster
  sugar
2 large eggs
125 g (4 oz)
  self-raising flour,
  sifted
4 tablespoons golden
  syrup
SAUCE:
4 tablespoons golden
  syrup
1 tablespoon water

Cream the butter or margarine and sugar together until light and fluffy. Beat in the eggs, one at a time, adding a little of the flour with the second egg. Fold in the remaining flour.

Butter a 900 ml (1½ pint) pudding basin and spoon in the syrup, then put the sponge mixture on top. Cover with buttered foil, making a pleat across the centre to allow the pudding to rise. Steam for 1½ to 2 hours.

To make the sauce: Heat the syrup and water in a small pan. Turn the pudding out onto a warmed serving dish and pour the hot sauce over before serving.
Serves 4

Chocolate Sponge Pudding

SPONGE MIXTURE:
175 g (6 oz)
   self-raising flour
2 tablespoons cocoa
   powder
125 g (4 oz) butter
   or margarine
125 g (4 oz) caster
   sugar
2 large eggs
2 tablespoons milk
CHOCOLATE SAUCE:
75 g (3 oz) plain
   chocolate, broken
   into pieces
3 tablespoons golden
   syrup
2 tablespoons water

Sift the flour and cocoa together. Cream the fat and sugar together until light and fluffy. Beat in the eggs, one at a time, adding a little of the flour and cocoa with the second egg. Fold in the remaining flour and cocoa, then mix in the milk.

Spoon the mixture into a buttered 1.2 litre (2 pint) pudding basin. Cover with buttered foil, making a pleat across the centre to allow the pudding to rise. Steam for 1½ to 2 hours.

To make the sauce: Melt the chocolate with the syrup and water in a small bowl over a pan of boiling water, then beat until smooth.

Turn the pudding out onto a warmed serving dish and pour the hot sauce over before serving.
Serves 4

Lemon Pudding

50 g (2 oz) butter or
   margarine
grated rind and juice
   of 1 large lemon
75 g (3 oz) caster
   sugar
2 eggs, separated
25 g (1 oz) plain
   flour, sifted
175 ml (6 fl oz)
   milk

Cream the butter or margarine with the lemon rind and sugar until light and fluffy. Mix in the egg yolks, flour and lemon juice, then gradually stir in the milk. Whisk the egg whites until stiff; fold into the mixture.

Turn into a greased 600 ml (1 pint) ovenproof dish and place in a roasting pan, containing 2.5 cm (1 inch) water.

Bake in a preheated moderate oven, 180°C (350°F), Gas Mark 4, for 40 to 45 minutes. Serve hot.
Serves 4

Blackberry and Apple Crumble

75 g (3 oz) butter
175 g (6 oz)
   wholewheat flour
75 g (3 oz) demerara
   sugar
500 g (1 lb) cooking
   apples, peeled,
   cored and sliced
250 g (8 oz)
   blackberries
75 g (3 oz) sugar

Rub the butter into the flour until the mixture resembles breadcrumbs, then stir in the demerara sugar.

Layer the apples, blackberries and sugar in a 900 ml (1½ pint) ovenproof dish.

Sprinkle the crumble mixture over the fruit to cover completely. Bake in a preheated moderate oven, 180°C (350°F), Gas Mark 4, for 40 to 50 minutes until golden brown.

Serve hot or cold with Crème à la Vanille (see page 58).
Serves 4 to 6

Bread and Butter Pudding

9 slices white bread,
  crusts removed
50 g (2 oz) butter
50 g (2 oz) sultanas
  or currants
50 g (2 oz) caster
  sugar
2 large eggs
600 ml (1 pint) milk
grated nutmeg

Spread the bread thickly with butter and cut each slice into 4. Arrange half in a buttered 1.2 litre (2 pint) ovenproof dish, buttered side down. Sprinkle with the fruit and half the sugar. Cover with remaining bread, butter side up.

Beat the eggs and milk together and strain over the pudding. Sprinkle with the remaining sugar and nutmeg to taste and leave for 30 minutes.

Bake in a preheated moderate oven, 160°C (325°F), Gas Mark 3, for 50 to 60 minutes until the top is golden. Serve with custard or cream.
Serves 4

Eve's Pudding

500 g (1 lb) cooking
    apples, peeled,
    cored and thinly
    sliced
50 g (2 oz) soft
    brown sugar
125 g (4 oz) butter
    or margarine
125 g (4 oz) caster
    sugar
2 eggs
125 g (4 oz)
    self-raising flour,
    sifted
1 tablespoon hot
    water

Put the apples in a greased 1.2 litre (2 pint) shallow ovenproof dish and sprinkle with the brown sugar.

Cream the butter or margarine with the caster sugar until light and fluffy. Add the eggs, one at a time, adding a little flour with the second egg. Fold in the remaining flour, then the hot water.

Spread the mixture evenly over the apples and bake in a preheated moderate oven, 180°C (350°F), Gas Mark 4, for 40 to 45 minutes until golden brown.

Serve with cream or custard.

Serves 4

Pineapple Pudding

1 x 439 g (15½ oz)
  can pineapple
  slices, drained
15 g (½ oz) angelica
125 g (4 oz) butter
  or margarine
125 g (4 oz) caster
  sugar
grated rind and juice
  of 1 lemon
2 eggs
150 g (5 oz)
  self-raising flour,
  sifted

Butter a 900 ml (1½ pint) pudding basin and arrange the pineapple slices around the base and sides. Place a piece of angelica in the centre of each.

Cream the butter or margarine, sugar and lemon rind together until light and fluffy. Add the eggs, one at a time, adding a little flour with the second egg. Beat thoroughly, then fold in the remaining flour with the lemon juice.

Turn the mixture into the basin. Cover with buttered foil, making a pleat across the centre to allow the pudding to rise. Steam for 1½ to 2 hours.

Turn out onto a warmed serving dish. Serve with Crème à la Vanille (see page 58).

Serves 4

Apricot Upside-Down Pudding

175 g (6 oz) butter
  or margarine
50 g (2 oz) soft
  brown sugar
1 x 411 g (14½ oz)
  can apricot halves,
  or cooked fresh
  apricots, halved and
  stoned
125 g (4 oz) caster
  sugar
2 eggs
125 g (4 oz)
  self-raising flour,
  sifted
1 teaspoon ground
  mixed spice

Cream 50 g (2 oz) of the fat, mix with the brown sugar and spread over the bottom of a 1.2 litre (2 pint) ovenproof dish. Drain the apricots, reserving 1 tablespoon juice. Arrange in the dish.

Cream the remaining fat with the caster sugar until light and fluffy. Add the eggs, one at a time, adding a tablespoon of the flour with the last two. Beat thoroughly, then fold in the remaining flour, mixed spice and reserved apricot juice.

Spread over the apricots and bake in a preheated moderate oven, 180°C (350°F), Gas Mark 4, for 55 to 60 minutes, until the sponge springs back when lightly pressed.

Turn out onto a warmed serving dish and serve with cream or Crème à la Vanille (see page 58).
Serves 6

Brown Betty

10 slices white bread,
    crusts removed
75 g (3 oz) butter
750 g-1 kg (1½-2 lb)
    cooking apples,
    peeled, cored and
    sliced
75 g (3 oz) soft
    brown sugar

Spread the bread thickly with butter and cut each slice into 4. Butter a 1.5 litre (2½ pint) ovenproof dish generously and line with some of the bread, butter side down.

Cover with half the apples, sprinkle with sugar and arrange another layer of bread over the top. Cover with the remaining apples, sprinkle with sugar and top with the remaining bread, butter side up and slightly overlapping. Sprinkle with the remaining sugar.

Cover with foil and bake in a preheated moderate oven, 180°C (350°F), Gas Mark 4, for 35 minutes. Remove the foil and bake for a further 5 minutes until crisp and golden. Serve hot with custard or cream.
Serves 6

Blackberry and Apple Layer

125 g (4 oz) butter
500 g (1 lb) cooking
apples, peeled,
cored and sliced
250 g (8 oz)
blackberries
75 g (3 oz) demerara
sugar
125 g (4 oz) fresh
breadcrumbs

Melt 25 g (1 oz) of the butter in a
pan. Add the apples, blackberries and
25 g (1 oz) of the sugar. Cover and
simmer gently until soft but not
pulpy.

Melt the remaining butter in a
frying pan and fry the breadcrumbs
until golden brown. Cool, then add
the remaining sugar.

Divide half the fruit between 4
individual glass dishes and cover
with half the crumbs, then repeat the
layers.

Serve chilled with whipped cream.
Serves 4

Christmas Pudding

175 g (6 oz) plain
flour
2 teaspoons ground
mixed spice
1 teaspoon ground
cinnamon
1/2 teaspoon grated
nutmeg
175 g (6 oz) fresh
white breadcrumbs
175 g (6 oz) butter
175 g (6 oz) soft
brown sugar
350 g (12 oz)
sultanas
250 g (8 oz) raisins
250 g (8 oz) currants
75 g (3 oz) chopped
mixed peel
grated rind and juice
of 1 orange
2 eggs, beaten
120 ml (4 fl oz)
brown ale

Sift the flour and spices into a bowl,
add the breadcrumbs, then rub in the
butter. Stir in the sugar, add the
remaining ingredients and mix
thoroughly.

Turn into a greased 1.75 litre
(3 pint) pudding basin, cover with
a pudding cloth or greaseproof paper
and foil, and steam for 6 hours,
topping up the pan with boiling
water as necessary.

Cool slightly, then remove the
cloth or paper and leave to cool
completely. Cover with clean
greaseproof paper and foil and store
in a cool dry place.

To serve, steam the pudding again
for 2 to 2 1/2 hours. Turn out onto a
warmed serving dish. If liked, pour
over 2 to 3 tablespoons warmed
brandy and ignite. Top with a sprig
of holly and serve with cream or
Brandy Butter.

Serves 8 to 10

NOTE: Christmas Pudding improves
with keeping as it allows the mixture
to mature. If possible, make it 3 to 4
months before Christmas.

Brandy Butter

150 g (6 oz)
  unsalted butter
150 g (6 oz) caster
  sugar
3-4 tablespoons
  brandy

Cream the butter until soft then gradually add the sugar and brandy, beating thoroughly with each addition.

Pile into a serving dish. Chill until firm.

Serves 8 to 10

75

SPECIAL OCCASION DESSERTS

Malakoff Gâteau

75 g (3 oz) butter
75 g (3 oz) caster
  sugar
1 egg yolk
125 g (4 oz) ground
  almonds
90 ml (3 fl oz)
  single cream
3 tablespoons brandy
300 ml (½ pint) cold
  strong black coffee
24 sponge fingers
150 ml (¼ pint)
  double cream,
  whipped
toasted flaked
  almonds to
  decorate

Cream the butter and sugar together until light and fluffy. Add the egg yolk, almonds and single cream and beat until smooth.

Add the brandy to the coffee and quickly dip the sponge fingers into it. Arrange some in the base of a lined and greased 500 g (1 lb) loaf tin.

Spread half the almond mixture on top. Repeat these layers once more, then finish with a layer of sponge fingers. Chill in the refrigerator until set.

Spread two-thirds of the cream over the gâteau. Pipe cream on top and sprinkle with almonds to decorate.
Serves 6 to 8

Zucotto

1 quantity chocolate
   sponge mixture
   (see method)
4 tablespoons brandy
450 ml (¾ pint)
   double cream
40 g (1½ oz) icing
   sugar, sifted
50 g (2 oz) plain
   chocolate, chopped
25 g (1 oz) almonds,
   chopped and
   toasted
175 g (6 oz) black
   cherries, stoned
2 tablespoons Kirsch
1 tablespoon cocoa
   powder, sifted

Prepare the sponge mixture as for
Black Forest Gâteau (see page 86).
Spoon into a lined and greased 20 cm
(8 inch) cake tin. Bake in a preheated
moderate oven, 180°C (350°F), Gas
Mark 4, for 35 to 40 minutes. Turn
onto a wire rack to cool.

Split the sponge in half and line a
1.2 litre (2 pint) pudding basin with
one layer, shaping it to fit. Sprinkle
the sides with the brandy; set aside.

Whip the cream until it forms soft
peaks. Fold in 25 g (1 oz) of the icing
sugar, the chocolate, almonds,
cherries and Kirsch. Spoon into the
basin and top with the remaining
sponge. Cover with a plate and chill
for 2 to 3 hours.

Run a palette knife around the
sides of the bowl and turn out onto a
plate. Sprinkle with the remaining
icing sugar and cocoa powder to make
a pattern.
Serves 6 to 8

Crêpes Suzette

BATTER:
125 g (4 oz) plain
flour
pinch of salt
1 egg, beaten
300 ml (½ pint)
milk
1 tablespoon oil
ORANGE SAUCE:
50 g (2 oz) butter
50 g (2 oz) caster
sugar
grated rind and juice
of 2 oranges
2 tablespoons Grand
Marnier
2 tablespoons brandy

Sift the flour and salt into a bowl and make a well in the centre. Add the egg, then gradually add half the milk, stirring constantly. Add the oil and beat thoroughly until smooth. Add the remaining milk and leave to stand for 30 minutes.

Heat a 15 cm (6 inch) omelet pan and add a few drops of oil. Pour in 1 tablespoon of batter and tilt the pan to coat the bottom evenly. Cook until the underside is brown, then turn over and cook for 10 seconds. Turn out onto a wire rack and cover with a tea towel. Repeat with the remaining batter, stacking the cooked pancakes one on top of the other.

To make the orange sauce: Melt the butter in a frying pan, add the sugar, orange rind and juice and heat until bubbling. Dip each crêpe into the sauce, fold into quarters then place in a warmed serving dish.

Add the Grand Marnier and brandy to the pan, heat gently, then ignite. Pour the flaming liquid over the crêpes and serve immediately.
Serves 4

Crêpes au Chocolat

BATTER:
125 g (4 oz) plain
 flour
pinch of salt
2 tablespoons caster
 sugar
1 tablespoon instant
 coffee powder
1 tablespoon cocoa
 powder
2 eggs, beaten
250 ml (8 fl oz)
 milk
1 tablespoon oil
SAUCE:
175 g (6 oz) plain
 chocolate, chopped
150 ml (¼ pint)
 water
1 teaspoon instant
 coffee powder
125 g (4 oz) sugar
FILLING:
284 ml (10 fl oz)
 double cream
2 tablespoons rum

Make and cook the pancakes as for
Crêpes Suzette (see opposite), sifting
the sugar, coffee and cocoa with the
flour and salt; set aside to cool.

To make the sauce: Place the
chocolate, 2 tablespoons of the water
and the coffee in a small pan and heat
gently until melted. Add the
remaining water and the sugar and
heat gently, stirring, until dissolved,
then simmer, uncovered, for 10
minutes. Leave to cool.

To make the filling: Whip the
cream until fairly stiff. Fold in the
rum.

Place a spoonful of cream on each
pancake, roll up and place on a
serving dish. Just before serving,
pour over a little chocolate sauce.
Serve the remaining sauce separately.
Serves 6

Raspberry Gâteau

3 eggs, separated
125 g (4 oz) caster
  sugar
grated rind and juice
  of ½ lemon
50 g (2 oz) semolina
25 g (1 oz) ground
  almonds
TO FINISH:
284 ml (10 fl oz)
  double cream,
  whipped
250 g (8 oz)
  raspberries
4 tablespoons
  redcurrant jelly
2 teaspoons water
50 g (2 oz) blanched
  almonds, chopped
  and toasted

Whisk the egg yolks with the sugar, lemon rind and juice until thick and creamy. Stir in the semolina and ground almonds. Whisk the egg whites until stiff and fold into the mixture.

Turn into a lined, greased and floured 20 cm (8 inch) sandwich tin. Bake in a preheated moderate oven, 180°C (350°F), Gas Mark 4, for 35 to 40 minutes. Turn onto a wire rack to cool.

Split the cake in half. Sandwich together with three-quarters of the cream. Arrange the raspberries on the top, leaving a border around the edge.

Heat the redcurrant jelly with the water. Use this glaze to brush the raspberries and the sides of the cake. Coat the sides with the almonds. Pipe the remaining cream around the top.
Serves 6

Strawberry Choux Ring

CHOUX PASTRY:
50 g (2 oz) butter or
  margarine
150 ml (¼ pint)
  water
65 g (2½ oz) plain
  flour, sifted
2 eggs, beaten
25 g (1 oz) flaked
  almonds
FILLING:
284 ml (10 fl oz)
  double cream
1 tablespoon caster
  sugar
350 g (12 oz)
  strawberries,
  halved
TO FINISH:
sifted icing sugar

Make the choux pastry as for Profiteroles (see opposite). Spoon onto a dampened baking sheet to form a 20 cm (8 inch) ring. Sprinkle with the almonds and bake in a preheated hot oven, 220°C (425°F), Gas Mark 7, for 15 minutes. Lower the heat to 190°C (375°F), Gas Mark 5, and bake for a further 20 to 25 minutes until golden brown. Cool on a wire rack.

Whip the cream until it holds its shape, then fold in the caster sugar and 250 g (8 oz) of the strawberries.

Split the ring in half horizontally and pile the filling into the hollow bottom half. Cover with the remaining strawberries then replace the top half of the choux ring. Sprinkle with icing sugar.
Serves 6

Profiteroles

CHOUX PASTRY:
50 g (2 oz) butter or
  margarine
150 ml (¼ pint)
  water
65 g (2½ oz) plain
  flour, sifted
2 eggs, beaten
CHOCOLATE SAUCE:
175 g (6 oz) plain
  chocolate
150 ml (¼ pint)
  water
1 teaspoon instant
  coffee powder
125 g (4 oz) sugar
FILLING:
1 tablespoon icing
  sugar, sifted
2-3 drops vanilla
  essence
170 ml (6 fl oz)
  double cream,
  whipped

Melt the fat in a large pan, add the water and bring to the boil. Add the flour all at once and beat until the mixture leaves the sides of the pan. Cool slightly, then add the eggs a little at a time, beating vigorously.

Put the mixture into a piping bag, fitted with a plain 1 cm (½ inch) nozzle, and pipe small mounds on a dampened baking sheet.

Bake in a preheated hot oven, 220°C (425°F), Gas Mark 7, for 10 minutes, then lower the heat to 190°C (375°F), Gas Mark 5, and bake for a further 20 to 25 minutes until golden. Make a slit in the side of each bun. Cool on a wire rack.

Make the chocolate sauce as for Crêpes au Chocolat (see page 79).

To make the filling: Fold the sugar and essence into the cream. Pipe or spoon a little into each profiterole.

Pile the profiteroles on a serving dish. Pour over the chocolate sauce.
Serves 4 to 6

Strawberry Shortcake

125 g (4 oz) butter
50 g (2 oz) caster
   sugar
125 g (4 oz) plain
   flour, sifted
50 g (2 oz)
   cornflour, sifted
250 g (8 oz)
   strawberries
284 ml (10 fl oz)
   double cream,
   whipped
sifted icing sugar for
   dredging

Cream the butter and sugar together until soft and creamy, then stir in the flour and cornflour. Mix to a firm dough, then turn onto a floured surface and knead lightly. Divide the mixture in half. Roll each piece into a 20 cm (8 inch) round on a baking sheet.

Bake in a preheated moderate oven, 180°C (350°F), Gas Mark 4, for 20 minutes. Leave for a few minutes, then mark one round into 6 sections. Carefully slide both rounds onto a wire rack to cool.

Slice the strawberries lengthwise. Set aside 6 slices for decoration. Mix three-quarters of the cream with the strawberries and spread over the plain round of shortcake. Break the other round into sections and place on top. Sprinkle with icing sugar. Pipe a cream rosette on each section and decorate with the reserved strawberry slices.

Serves 6

Hazelnut Meringue

4 egg whites
275 g (9 oz) caster
   sugar
few drops of vanilla
   essence
1 teaspoon vinegar
125 g (4 oz) ground
   hazelnuts, toasted
FILLING:
284 ml (10 fl oz)
   double cream,
   whipped
1 tablespoon caster
   sugar
250 g (8 oz)
   raspberries
TO FINISH:
sifted icing sugar

Whisk the egg whites until stiff, then whisk in the sugar, a tablespoon at a time. Continue whisking until the meringue is very stiff and holds its shape. Carefully fold in the vanilla essence, vinegar and hazelnuts.

Divide the mixture between two lined and greased 20 cm (8 inch) sandwich tins and spread evenly. Bake in a preheated moderate oven, 180°C (350°F), Gas Mark 4, for 40 to 45 minutes.

Loosen from the tin with a sharp knife and turn onto a wire rack to cool.

To make the filling: Mix two-thirds of the cream with the sugar and raspberries, reserving a few for decoration. Sandwich the meringue rounds together with the filling and dust the top with icing sugar.

Decorate with piped cream rosettes and the reserved raspberries.
Serves 6

Vacherin aux Marrons

5 egg whites
300 g (10 oz) caster
sugar
FILLING:
450 ml (³/4 pint)
double cream
227 g (8 oz) can
sweetened chestnut
purée
2 tablespoons brandy
TO DECORATE:
sifted icing sugar
25 g (1 oz) grated
chocolate

Whisk the egg whites until stiff, then whisk in 3 tablespoons of the sugar. Carefully fold in the remaining sugar.

Put the meringue into a piping bag, fitted with a 1 cm (½ inch) plain nozzle. Pipe into three 20 cm (8 inch) rounds on baking sheets lined with silicone paper. Bake in a preheated cool oven, 140°C (275°F), Gas Mark 1, for 1½ to 2 hours. Peel off the paper and cool on a wire rack.

Whip the cream until it holds its shape. Combine three-quarters of the cream with the chestnut purée and brandy. Sandwich the meringue rounds together with this mixture.

Sprinkle with icing sugar and decorate with grated chocolate. Pipe cream around the edge.
Serves 8

Meringue Baskets

MERINGUE:
4 egg whites
few drops of vanilla
    essence
275 g (9 oz) icing
    sugar, sifted
FILLING:
150 ml (¼ pint)
    double cream,
    whipped
125 g (4 oz)
    strawberries
2 tablespoons
    redcurrant jelly,
    warmed

Whisk the egg whites until stiff, then whisk in the vanilla essence and the icing sugar, a tablespoon at a time. Place the bowl over a pan of gently simmering water and continue whisking for about 5 minutes until the meringue is very stiff.

Line a baking sheet with silicone paper and draw eight 7.5 cm (3 inch) circles on the paper. Spread half the meringue over the circles to form bases. Put the remaining meringue into a piping bag, fitted with a large fluted nozzle, and pipe round the edge of each base.

Bake in a preheated cool oven, 150°C (300°F), Gas Mark 2, for 1 to 1¼ hours. Cool on a wire rack. Remove the paper.

Spoon a little cream into each basket and arrange the strawberries on top. Brush the redcurrant jelly over the strawberries to glaze.
Makes 8

Black Forest Gâteau

SPONGE MIXTURE:
3 large eggs
75 g (3 oz) caster
  sugar
50 g (2 oz) plain
  flour
1 tablespoon cocoa
  powder
1 tablespoon oil
TO FINISH:
1 x 425 g (15 oz)
  can black cherries
1 tablespoon
  arrowroot
3 tablespoons Kirsch
284 ml (10 fl oz)
  double cream,
  whipped
chocolate curls (see
  page 65)

Place the eggs and sugar in a bowl and whisk over a pan of simmering water until thick and mousse-like. Sift the flour with the cocoa and fold in, then fold in the oil.

Turn into a lined and greased 20 cm (8 inch) round cake tin. Bake in a preheated moderately hot oven, 190°C (375°F), Gas Mark 5, for 30 to 35 minutes. Cool on a wire rack.

Drain the cherries and mix a little of the juice with the arrowroot in a small bowl. Pour the remaining juice into a pan and bring to the boil. Pour onto the arrowroot and stir well. Return to the pan and heat gently, stirring until thick and clear. Stone the cherries, add to the pan and cool.

Slice the cake in half horizontally and sprinkle both layers with Kirsch. Place one layer on a plate, and pipe a line of cream around the top edge. Spread the cherry mixture in the centre and top with the other layer.

Spread half the remaining cream around the side of the gâteau and press chocolate curls into it. Pipe the remaining cream on top of the gâteau.
Serves 6

Crème Brûlée

4 egg yolks
1 tablespoon caster
  sugar
2 x 284 ml (10 fl oz)
  cartons double cream
few drops of vanilla
  essence
TO FINISH:
50 g (2 oz) caster
  sugar

Beat the egg yolks and sugar together. Warm the cream in a double saucepan, or bowl over a pan of simmering water. Carefully stir in the egg mixture. Continue cooking gently, stirring constantly, until thickened enough to coat the back of a spoon. Add the vanilla essence.

Strain into 6 ramekin dishes and place in a roasting pan, containing 2.5 cm (1 inch) water. Place in a preheated cool oven, 140°C (275°F), Gas Mark 1, for 30 to 40 minutes.

Remove the dishes from the pan cool then chill in the refrigerator overnight.

To finish: Sprinkle evenly with sugar. Place under a preheated hot grill until the sugar has caramelized. Cool, then chill in the refrigerator for 2 hours before serving.
Serves 6

Strawberry Mille Feuille

1 x 368 g (13 oz)
  packet frozen puff
  pastry, thawed
500 g (1 lb)
  strawberries
284 ml (10 fl oz)
  double cream,
  whipped
1 tablespoon icing
  sugar, sifted
4 tablespoons
  redcurrant jelly
2 teaspoons water
50 g (2 oz) almonds,
  finely chopped and
  toasted

Divide the pastry into 3 equal pieces and roll each into a rectangle, about 15 x 35 cm (6 x 14 inches). Place on dampened baking sheets, prick well all over and chill for 15 minutes.

Bake in a preheated hot oven, 220°C (425°F), Gas Mark 7, for 12 to 15 minutes until golden. Turn the pastry over and bake for 5 minutes.

Cool on a wire rack. Trim the edges to neaten; crush the trimmings.

Slice half the strawberries; halve the remainder and set aside. Fold the sliced strawberries into the cream with the icing sugar. Spread half the mixture onto one piece of the pastry. Place a second layer of pastry on top, spread with the remaining mixture and cover with the last piece of pastry.

Heat the redcurrant jelly with the water. Brush the top of the pastry with this glaze and arrange the remaining strawberries on top. Brush with glaze.

Mix the crushed pastry with the almonds and use to cover the sides.
Serves 8

Austrian Curd Cake

75 g (3 oz) butter

175 g (6 oz)
    digestive biscuits,
    crushed

50 g (2 oz) demerara
    sugar

350 g (12 oz) curd
    cheese

50 g (2 oz) caster
    sugar

3 eggs, separated

grated rind of
    1 lemon

15 g (½ oz) gelatine,
    soaked in 3 table-
    spoons water

450 ml (¾ pint)
    whipping cream,
    whipped

Melt the butter in a pan; mix in the biscuit crumbs and demerara sugar. Spread half the mixture over the base of a 20 cm (8 inch) loose-bottomed cake tin and chill in the refrigerator until firm.

Meanwhile, place the cheese in a bowl and beat in the sugar, egg yolks and lemon rind. Stir the soaked gelatine in a bowl over a pan of hot water until dissolved, then stir into the cheese mixture.

Fold two-thirds of the cream into the cheese mixture. Whisk the egg whites until stiff and fold into the mixture. Spoon over the biscuit base and place in the refrigerator for 10 minutes. Spread the remaining crumbs over the top and chill in the refrigerator for 2 hours.

Remove from the tin and decorate with piped cream.

Serves 8

Gâteau aux Noix

MERINGUE:
4 egg whites
250 g (8 oz) caster
  sugar
125 g (4 oz) walnut
  halves, ground
FILLING:
125 g (4 oz) sugar
4 tablespoons water
4 tablespoons hot
  black coffee
450 ml (¾ pint)
  double cream,
  whipped
TO FINISH:
sifted icing sugar
8 walnut halves

Whisk the egg whites until stiff, then whisk in 2 tablespoons of the caster sugar. Carefully fold in the remaining sugar with the walnuts.

Put the meringue into a piping bag, fitted with a 1 cm (½ inch) plain nozzle, and pipe into two 20 cm (8 inch) rounds on baking sheets lined with silicone paper. Bake in a preheated cool oven, 140°C (275°F), Gas Mark 1, for 1½ to 2 hours. Transfer to a wire rack to cool.

Place the sugar and water in a pan and heat gently until dissolved. Increase the heat and cook to a rich brown caramel. Remove from the heat, carefully add the coffee and stir until the caramel has melted, heating again if necessary, then cool.

Fold the cream into the caramel and use three-quarters to sandwich the meringue rounds together. Sprinkle the top with icing sugar. Pipe cream rosettes around the edge and decorate with walnut halves.
Serves 6

Hazelnut Galette

HAZELNUT PASTRY:
75 g (3 oz) butter
50 g (2 oz) caster sugar
125 g (4 oz) plain flour, sifted
75 g (3 oz) hazelnuts, ground and toasted

FILLING:
1 tablespoon apricot jam
500 g (1 lb) dessert apples, peeled, cored and sliced
25 g (1 oz) sultanas
25 g (1 oz) currants
1 teaspoon ground mixed spice
150 ml (¼ pint) double cream, whipped

TO FINISH:
sifted icing sugar
8 hazelnuts, toasted and skinned

Beat the butter and sugar together until light and fluffy. Stir in the flour and hazelnuts and mix to a firm dough, using one hand. Turn onto a floured surface and knead lightly until smooth. Divide the mixture in half and roll each piece into a 20 cm (8 inch) round on a baking sheet.

Bake in a preheated moderately hot oven, 190°C (375°F), Gas Mark 5, for 15 to 20 minutes until golden. Cut one round into 8 sections while still warm. Transfer both rounds to a wire rack to cool.

Place the jam and apples in a pan, cover and cook gently for 15 to 20 minutes until softened, stirring occasionally. Add the sultanas, currants and spice. Leave until cool.

Spread the cooled apple mixture over the hazelnut round. Cover with half the cream. Arrange the hazelnut sections on top and sprinkle with icing sugar. Pipe a cream rosette on each section and top with hazelnuts.
Serves 8

91

Apple Pancakes

PANCAKES:

125 g (4 oz) plain flour

pinch of salt

1 egg, beaten

300 ml (½ pint) milk

1 tablespoon oil

FILLING:

25 g (1 oz) butter

750 g (1½ lb) cooking apples, peeled, cored and sliced

50 g (2 oz) brown sugar

½ teaspoon ground cinnamon

50 g (2 oz) sultanas

TO FINISH:

3 tablespoons apricot jam, warmed

25 g (1 oz) flaked almonds, toasted

Make and cook the pancakes as for Crêpes Suzette (see page 78).

Melt the butter in a pan. Add the apples, sugar, cinnamon and sultanas. Cover and simmer gently for 10 to 15 minutes, until the apples are tender.

Place a pancake on a greased ovenproof dish, cover with some of the apple mixture, then another pancake. Continue in this way until the apple mixture and pancakes are all used, finishing with a pancake.

Spoon over the apricot jam to glaze. Bake in a preheated moderate oven, 180°C (350°F), Gas Mark 4, for 10 to 15 minutes until heated through.

Cut into wedges and sprinkle with almonds. Serve with whipped cream if liked.

Serves 6

Mocha Roulade

175 g (6 oz) plain
   chocolate
3 tablespoons water
1 tablespoon instant
   coffee powder
5 eggs, separated
250 g (8 oz) caster
   sugar
FILLING:
1 tablespoon instant
   coffee powder
1 tablespoon boiling
   water
284 ml (10 fl oz)
   double cream,
   whipped
1 tablespoon icing
   sugar
TO FINISH:
sifted icing sugar

Place the chocolate, water and coffee in a pan and heat gently until the chocolate has melted. Beat the egg yolks with the caster sugar until thick and creamy, then fold in the warm chocolate mixture.

Whisk the egg whites until stiff and fold into the chocolate mixture. Turn into a lined and greased 20 × 30 cm (8 × 12 inch) Swiss roll tin. Bake in a preheated moderate oven, 180°C (350°F), Gas Mark 4, for 20 to 25 minutes until firm.

Leave in the tin for 5 minutes, then cover with a clean damp cloth. Leave in the refrigerator overnight.

Carefully remove the cloth and turn the roulade out onto a sheet of greaseproof paper, sprinkled thickly with icing sugar. Peel off the lining paper.

Dissolve the coffee in the water, cool, then fold into the cream with the sugar. Spread evenly over the roulade and roll up like a Swiss roll. Transfer to a serving dish.
Serves 8

INDEX

Acknowledgments

Photography by Paul Williams
Food prepared by Carole Handslip
Designed by Astrid Publishing Consultants Ltd